STARS LIKE US

LELAND
MELVIN

The subject of this Reader Choice title was chosen by readers and educators. We are proud to bring you titles, topics, and stories that reflect the choices and voices of our diverse and brilliant readers!

BY J. P.

ILLUSTRA
AMANDA QUARTEY

Rourke
Educational Media

A Division of
Carson
Dellosa
Education

ROURKE'S
SCHOOL to HOME
CONNECTIONS
BEFORE AND DURING READING ACTIVITIES

Before Reading: *Building Background Knowledge and Vocabulary*

Building background knowledge can help children process new information and build upon what they already know. Before reading a book, it is important to tap into what children already know about the topic. This will help them develop their vocabulary and increase their reading comprehension.

Questions and Activities to Build Background Knowledge:

1. Look at the front cover of the book and read the title. What do you think this book will be about?
2. What do you already know about this topic?
3. Take a book walk and skim the pages. Look at the table of contents, photographs, captions, and bold words. Did these text features give you any information or predictions about what you will read in this book?

Vocabulary: *Vocabulary Is Key to Reading Comprehension*

Use the following directions to prompt a conversation about each word.

- Read the vocabulary words.
- What comes to mind when you see each word?
- What do you think each word means?

> ### Vocabulary Words:
> - astronaut
> - athlete
> - crew
> - draft
> - equipment
> - experiments
> - exploration
> - laboratory

During Reading: *Reading for Meaning and Understanding*

To achieve deep comprehension of a book, children are encouraged to use close reading strategies. During reading, it is important to have children stop and make connections. These connections result in deeper analysis and understanding of a book.

 Close Reading a Text

During reading, have children stop and talk about the following:

- Any confusing parts
- Any unknown words
- Text to text, text to self, text to world connections
- The main idea in each chapter or heading

Encourage children to use context clues to determine the meaning of any unknown words. These strategies will help children learn to analyze the text more thoroughly as they read.

When you are finished reading this book, turn to the next-to-last page for **Text-Dependent Questions** and an **Extension Activity**.

TABLE OF CONTENTS

5, 4, 3, 2, 1...
LIFTOFF!

Have you ever wanted to visit a new place? How would you get there? Leland Melvin wanted to go to outer space. He joined the **astronaut** program at the National Aeronautics and Space Administration (NASA). He was a leader in space **exploration**. Now, his dream was about to come true. He was on the space shuttle *Atlantis* waiting to launch.

The shuttle crew fastened Leland's harness. The clock ticked as rockets roared. It was an important day for him. He would be making his first trip as an astronaut.

A GIANT IN THE SKY

The *Atlantis* space shuttle had three parts: an outside tank, two booster rockets, and the orbiter. The *Atlantis* weighed 4.5 million pounds (over 2 million kilograms) and carried 4 million pounds (over 1.8 million kilograms) of fuel.

Leland happily bumped fists with his **crew** members. They would be living and working together in space for the next two weeks.

"...liftoff!"

In no time, the shuttle was miles above Earth. Leland looked out the window into the dark sky. He had never seen anything so beautiful.

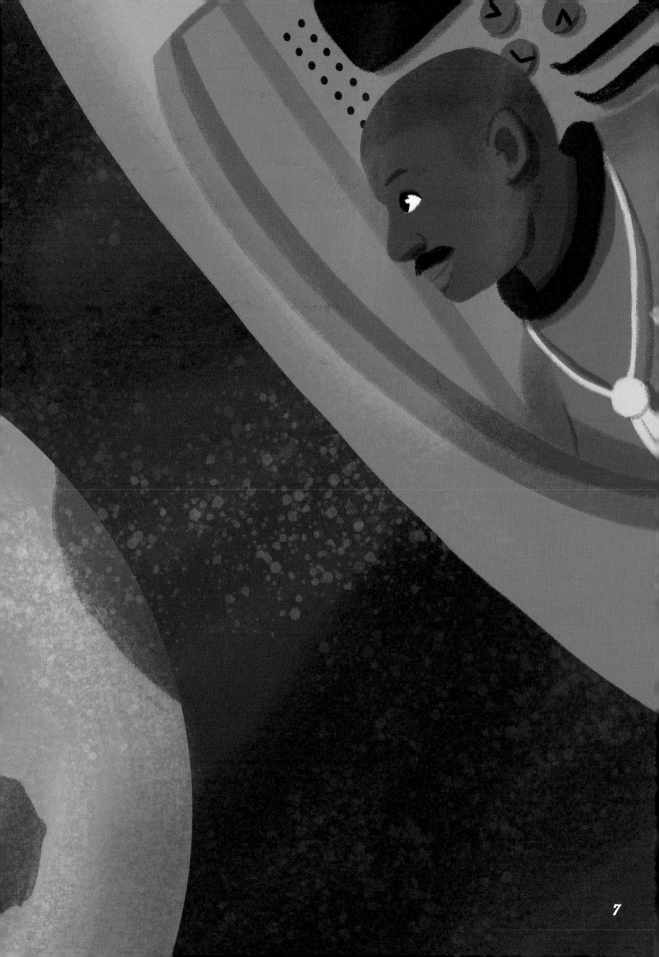

SPORTS AND SCIENCE

Leland loved science as a kid. He enjoyed doing **experiments** at home. In high school, he took advanced classes. Leland also loved sports. He was a star player for his high school football team. Being a great **athlete** earned him a scholarship to the University of Richmond.

Leland kept playing football and studying science in college. After he graduated, he wanted to play football professionally. He hoped he would be picked for the 1986 National Football League (NFL) **draft**. The Detroit Lions asked him to join them. With that, Leland became an NFL player.

Leland went to Michigan to train in the spring. One day, he was running when he felt something snap in his leg. He fell to the ground in pain. He took a break from football because of this injury. Leland returned to Virginia. His leg healed. He began training again, but for a different team. He still wanted to play football, but he was hurt a second time and had to quit.

Leland had a new plan: he would go back to college and become a scientist. He worked hard and became an expert in space. He began working for NASA. While there, he applied to be an astronaut and was accepted.

To go to space, Leland needed to do a lot of training. He was ready for this new adventure. Part of his training was swimming in a pool in a spacesuit to feel what it was like in space.

Leland was lowered into a swimming pool. He started to train, but his suit was missing an important piece of **equipment**. His ears started to hurt, and he could not hear. After he got out of the water, doctors discovered that he had an ear injury. They said that he could lose his hearing forever. Even worse, he could not go to space if his hearing did not come back. But Leland did not give up on his dream.

Leland worked for NASA while waiting for his hearing to come back. He helped people learn about space. One day, a wonderful thing happened. A doctor checked Leland's ear and discovered that the injury had healed. The doctor gave Leland permission to continue training. Leland's dream could come true after all.

AN ASTRONAUT AFTER ALL

Leland finished his training and became an astronaut. His first mission would be aboard the space shuttle *Atlantis*. It would take him to the *International Space Station* (*ISS*). There, he could help attach a new **laboratory** to the *ISS*. He would be working with astronauts from around the world.

FLYING THROUGH SPACE

Spacecraft move very quickly when in orbit. The *Atlantis* could travel 17,000 miles (over 27,350 kilometers) per hour.

There was a lot to do on the mission. The *Atlantis* crew **fixed the space station...**

...did experiments...

...and worked long days.

They enjoyed their free time, too. They even played catch on the space shuttle! Leland became the only person to catch a football in the NFL and in space.

Leland completed two space missions. He has spent over 565 hours in space! When he came back to Earth, he knew he wanted to help people learn about science.

Leland became the leader of NASA's Education Design Team. He helped improve the way that we teach people about space. He also helped run one of the US government's science education programs.

Leland was a leader in science. People hadn't forgotten about his football career, though. The Pro Football Hall of Fame honored him by putting his Detroit Lions football jersey in their museum.

Educating the next generation of astronauts became Leland's new life purpose. He retired from NASA in 2014. He now travels the world telling his story about being a leader and encouraging young learners.

“ The key to life is to never stop exploring. Whether it's exploring music, food, cultures... Everything is part of the journey, and it starts with exploration. ”

—Leland Melvin

TIME LINE

1964 Leland Melvin is born on February 15th to Deems and Grace Melvin in Lynchburg, Virginia.

1982 Leland plays wide receiver on the University of Richmond Spiders football team from 1982 to 1985.

1986 Leland is picked in the 11th round of the NFL draft to play for the Detroit Lions. He is injured in training camp.

1987 Leland reports to the Dallas Cowboys NFL team for spring training. His football career ends due to injuries.

1991 Leland earns a master of science degree in materials science engineering from the University of Virginia.

2008 Leland is a mission specialist aboard the space shuttle *Atlantis* mission STS-122 that is launched on February 8th.

2009 Leland is a Mission Specialist 1 aboard the space shuttle *Atlantis* mission STS-129 that is launched on November 16th.

2010 Leland is assigned to the Office of Education at NASA Headquarters and asked to lead the Education Design Team.

2014 Leland retires from NASA.

2015 Leland serves as the co-chair on the White House's Federal Coordination in STEM Education Task Force.

2018 Leland's memoir, *Chasing Space*, is released.

2019 Leland Melvin is honored by the Pro Football Hall of Fame for his athletic and academic accomplishments. They place his #4 Detroit Lions jersey on display in Canton, Ohio

GLOSSARY

astronaut (AS-truh-nawt): someone who travels in a spacecraft

athlete (ATH-leet): someone who is trained in or very good at sports and physical exercise

crew (kroo): a team of people who work together on a ship, an aircraft, or a specific job

draft: a process in which members of a professional sports team are selected

equipment (i-KWIP-muhnt): the tools, machines, or products needed for a particular purpose

experiments (ik-SPER-uh-ments): tests to try out a theory or to see the effect of something

exploration (ek-spluh-RAY-shuhn): the act of studying an unknown thing or place

laboratory (LAB-ruh-tor-ee): a room or building that has special equipment for people to use in scientific experiments

INDEX

TEXT-DEPENDENT QUESTIONS

1. How did Leland Melvin start his football career?

2. What were the different parts of the *Atlantis* space shuttle?

3. How did Leland Melvin temporarily lose his hearing?

4. What was one reason Leland Melvin and his crew went to outer space in the *Atlantis*?

5. What jobs did Leland Melvin have after he was an astronaut?

EXTENSION ACTIVITY

Learn more about being a scientist in space. Research one kind of technology that astronauts use when they are on missions. Think about what it does and how it is made. Build a model or a version of the technology that can be used on Earth. Try using your new technology and find one way to improve it.

ABOUT THE AUTHOR

J. P. Miller Growing up, J. P. Miller loved reading stories that she could become immersed in. As a writer, she enjoys doing the same for her readers. Through the gift of storytelling, she is able to bring little- and well-known people and events in African American history to life for young readers. She hopes that her stories will augment the classroom experience and inspire her readers. J. P. lives in metro Atlanta and is the author of the *Careers in the US Military* and *Black Stories Matter* series.

ABOUT THE ILLUSTRATOR

Amanda Quartey Amanda lives in the UK and was born and bred in London. She has always loved to draw and has been doing so ever since she can remember. At the age of 14, she moved to Ghana and studied art in school. She later returned to the UK to study graphic design. Her artistic path deviated slightly when she studied Classics at her university. Over the years, in a bid to return to her artistic roots, Amanda has built a professional illustration portfolio and is now loving every bit of her illustration career.

www.rourkeeducationalmedia.com

Quote source: CBS News, "Leland Melvin's inspiring story of rocketing across careers," YouTube video, 4:08, January 10, 2019, https://youtu.be/eqlHNCzNmUk.

Edited by: Tracie Santos
Illustrations by: Amanda Quartey
Cover and interior layout by: J.J. Giddings

Library of Congress PCN Data

Leland Melvin / J. P. Miller
(Leaders Like Us)
ISBN 978-1-73164-929-4 (hard cover)
ISBN 978-1-73164-877-8 (soft cover)
ISBN 978-1-73164-981-2 (e-Book)
ISBN 978-1-73165-033-7 (ePub)
Library of Congress Control Number: 2021935449

Rourke Educational Media
Printed in the United States of America
01-1872111937